Gerald Goehring Roy Miller Michael F. Mitri Pat Flicker Addiss Peter Billingsley

Timothy Laczynski Mariano Tolentino Louise H. Beard Michael Filerman Scott Hart
Bob Bartner Michael Jenkins Angela Milonas Bradford W. Smith

Present

A CHRISTMAS STORY
The Musical

Book by
Joseph Robinette

Music and Lyrics by
Benj Pasek and **Justin Paul**

Based upon the motion picture "**A Christmas Story**"
© 1983 Turner Entertainment Co., distributed by **Warner Bros.**
written by **Jean Shepherd, Leigh Brown** and **Bob Clark**
and "**In God We Trust All Others Pay Cash**" by **Jean Shepherd**
Produced with permission of **Warner Bros. Theatre Ventures, Inc.** and **Dalfie Entertainment, Inc.**

Starring
Dan Lauria

John Bolton

Johnny Rabe   Zac Ballard

and **Erin Dilly**

with

Tia Altinay   John Babbo   Charissa Bertels   Grace Capeless   Zoe Considine
Andrew Cristi   Mathew deGuzman   Thay Floyd   George Franklin   Nick Gaswirth
Mark Ledbetter   Jose Luaces   Jack Mastrianni   Mara Newbery   Lindsay O'Neil
Sarah Min-Kyung Park   J.D. Rodriguez   Analise Scarpaci   Lara Seibert   Jeremy Shinder
Luke Spring   Beatrice Tulchin   Joe West   Kirsten Wyatt   and Eddie Korbich as Santa
and
Caroline O'Connor as Miss Shields

Set Design	Costume Design	Lighting Design	Sound Design
Walt Spangler	**Elizabeth Hope Clancy**	**Howell Binkley**	**Ken Travis**

Hair & Wig Design	Animals by	Associate Choreographer	Casting
Tom Watson	**William Berloni Theatrical Animals, Inc.**	**James Gray**	**Stephanie Klapper, CSA**

Vocal Arrangements	Music Coordinator	Production Stage Manager	Technical Supervisor
Justin Paul	**Talitha Fehr**	**Peter Wolf**	**Fred Gallo**

General Management	Press Representative	Advertising & Marketing	Associate Producers
Corker Group, LLC John S. Corker	**Keith Sherman & Associates**	**aka**	**Dancap Productions, Inc. Jeffrey Jackson Ric Zivic**

Orchestrations	Music Direction and Supervision	Dance Music Arrangements
Larry Blank	**Ian Eisendrath**	**Glen Kelly**

Choreographed by
Warren Carlyle

Directed by
John Rando

World premiere produced by Kansas City Repertory Theatre, Eric Rosen, Artistic Director
Jerry Genochio, Producing Director; Cynthia Rider, Managing Director
Subsequently produced by The 5th Avenue Theatre, Seattle, Washington, David Armstrong, Executive Producer and Artistic Director,
Bernadine C. Griffin, Managing Director and Bill Berry, Producing Director

ISBN 978-1-4768-4725-8

Visit Hal Leonard Online at
www.halleonard.com

World headquarters, contact:
Hal Leonard
7777 West Bluemound Road
Milwaukee, WI 53213
Email: info@halleonard.com

In Europe, contact:
Hal Leonard Europe Limited
Dettingen Way
Bury St. Edmunds, Suffolk, IP33 3YB
Email: info@halleonardeurope.com

In Australia, contact:
Hal Leonard Australia Pty. Ltd.
4 Lentara Court
Cheltenham, Victoria, 3192 Australia
Email: info@halleonard.com.au

A KID AT CHRISTMAS

Words and Music by BENJ PASEK
and JUSTIN PAUL

COUNTING DOWN TO CHRISTMAS

Words and Music by BENJ PASEK
and JUSTIN PAUL

RALPHIE:

'Cause this year, _____ don't need an - oth - er plaid tie.

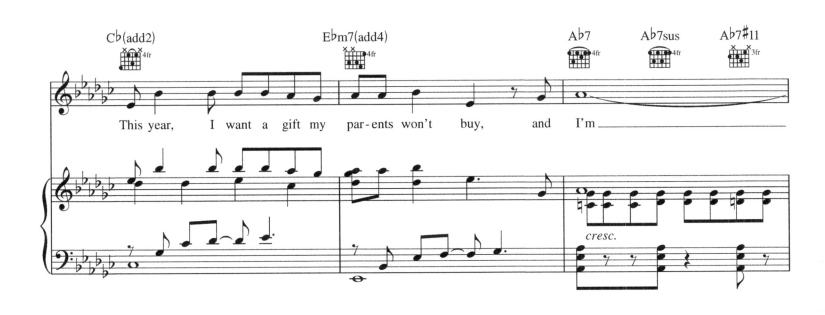

This year, I want a gift my par - ents won't buy, and I'm _____

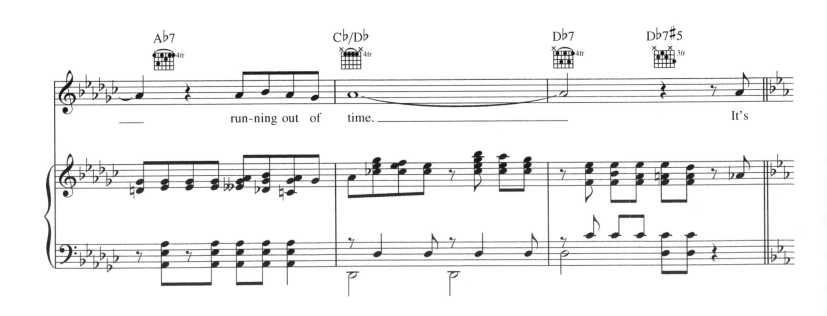

_____ run-ning out of time. _____ It's

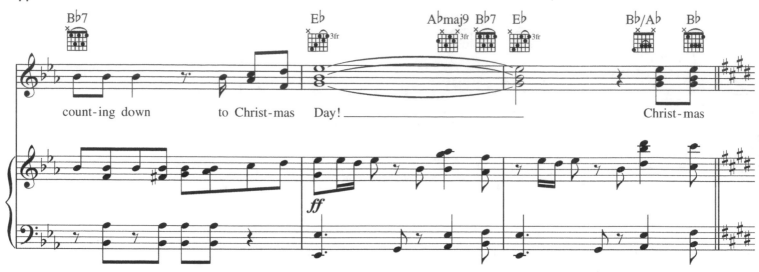

count-ing down   to Christ-mas Day! _____   Christ-mas

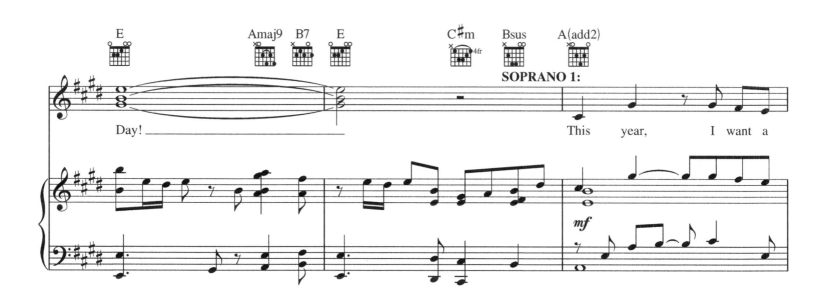

Day! _____   SOPRANO 1:   This   year,   I want a

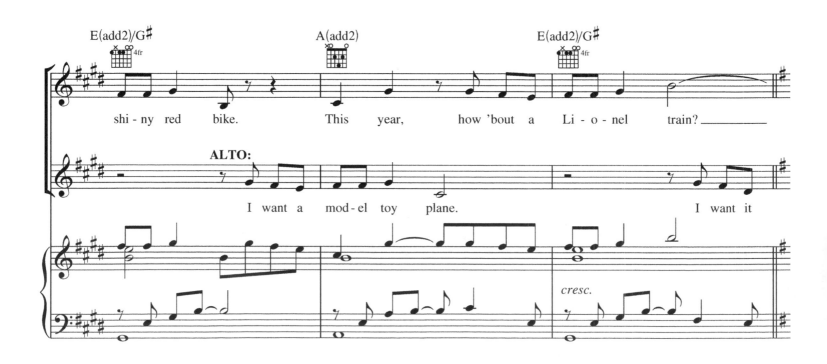

shi-ny red   bike.   This   year,   how 'bout a Li-o-nel   train? _____

ALTO:

I want a mod-el toy   plane.   I want it

cresc.

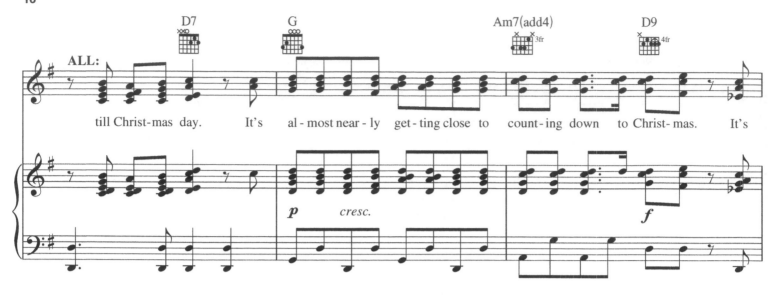

till Christ-mas day. It's al-most near-ly get-ting close to count-ing down to Christ-mas. It's

al-most time to see the tree light up the town for Christ-mas. It's thir-ty-four thou-sand,

for-ty-eight min-utes a - way.

RED RYDER® CARBINE ACTION BB GUN

Words and Music by BENJ PASEK
and JUSTIN PAUL

When you're big and brave like me no bul - ly can ev - er make fun! My mom is cry - in', "Cow - boy

Ralph - ie!" while my Dad is yell - in', "That boy, he's my __

__ son!" __

With a Red Ry - der Car - bine Ac - tion B - B

Gun. __

But it's al - most near - ly get - ting close,

THE GENIUS ON CLEVELAND STREET

Words and Music by BENJ PASEK
and JUSTIN PAUL

WHEN YOU'RE A WIMP

Words and Music by BENJ PASEK
and JUSTIN PAUL

RALPHIE TO THE RESCUE

Words and Music by BENJ PASEK
and JUSTIN PAUL

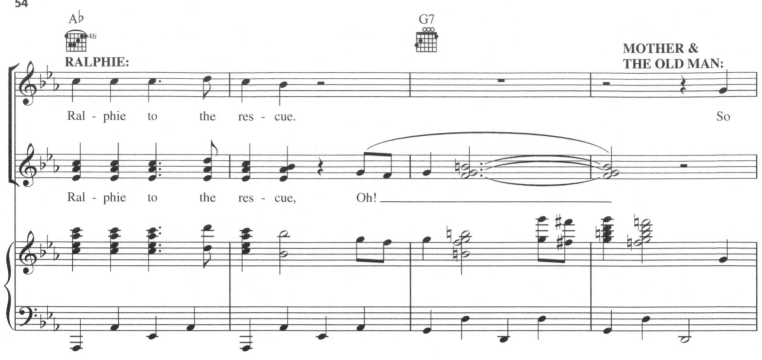

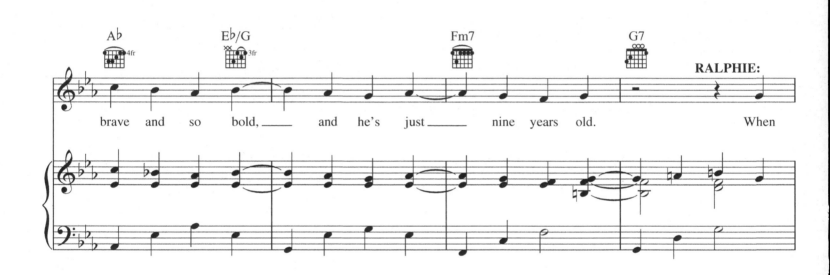

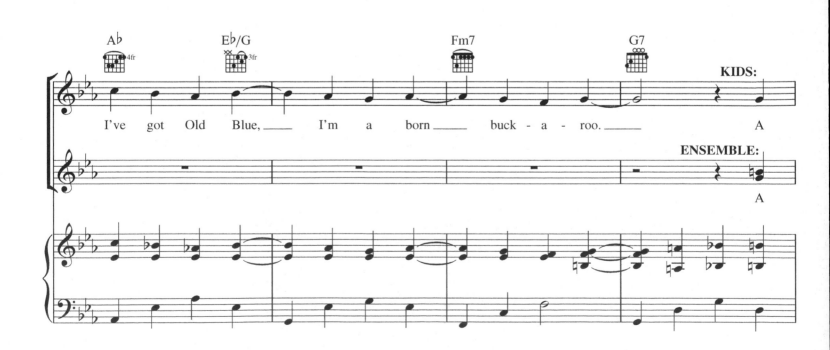

WHAT A MOTHER DOES

Words and Music by BENJ PASEK
and JUSTIN PAUL

MOTHER: New stains on the rug, stray socks on the stair,

61

JUST LIKE THAT

Words and Music by BENJ PASEK
and JUSTIN PAUL

SOMEWHERE HOVERING OVER INDIANA

Words and Music by BENJ PASEK
and JUSTIN PAUL

"Ho, ho, ho!" 'Cause I know some - where hov - er - ing o -

- ver In - di - an - a _____

San - ta's cov - er - ing ground ___ with light - ning speed.

High a - bove the town, fly - ing down, bet - ter

A CHRISTMAS STORY

Words and Music by BENJ PASEK
and JUSTIN PAUL

THE OLD MAN:
What a per - fect scene on a Christ - mas night. So we might be stuck with duck, but the world's al - right. And you have to

MOTHER:

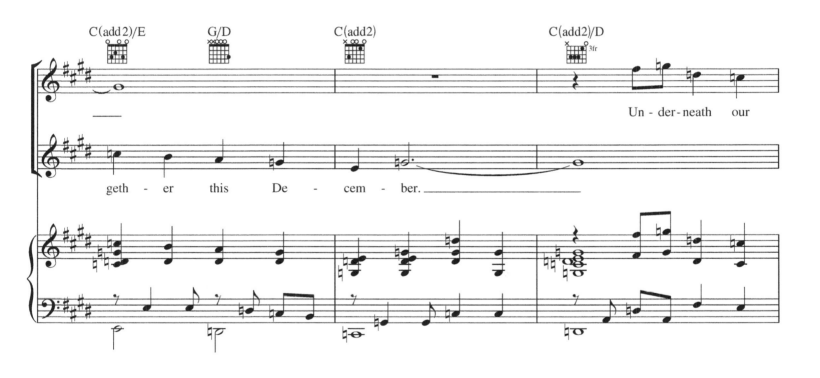

SOPRANOS & TENORS:

heart so full of joy. _____ From

ALTOS AND BARITONES:

We'll look back some - day, from

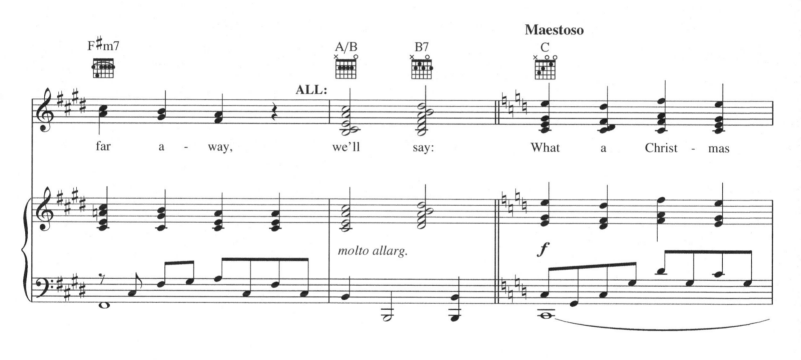

far a - way, we'll say: What a Christ - mas

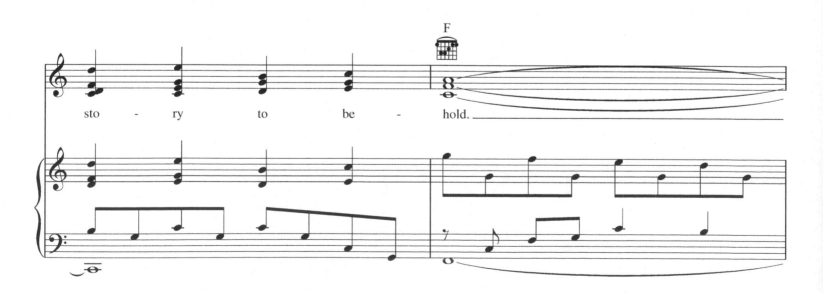

sto - ry to be - hold. _____

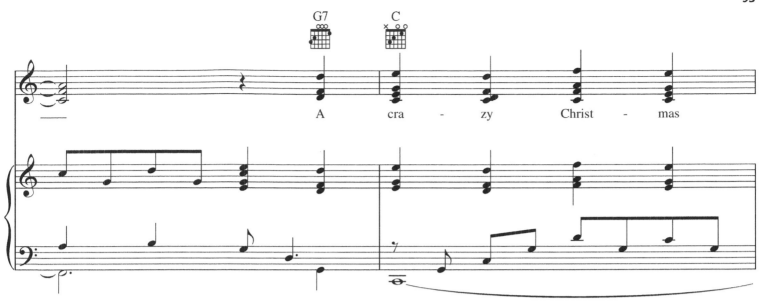

A cra - zy Christ - mas

Sto - ry to be told.

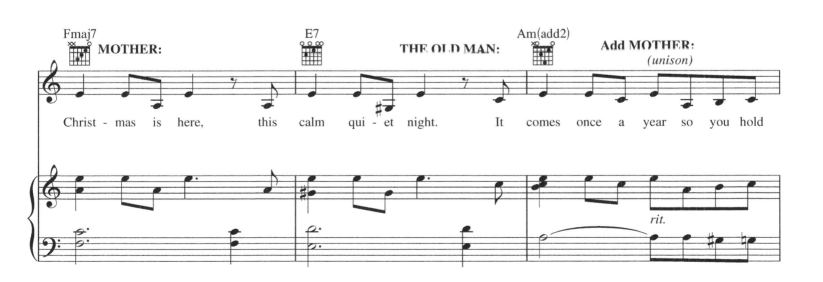

MOTHER:
Christ - mas is here, this calm qui - et night.

THE OLD MAN:
It comes once a year so you hold

Add MOTHER:
(unison)